Earth Then and Now

Activity Book

| Name: |
| Age: |
| Class: |
| School: |

UNIVERSITY PRESS

Great Clarendon Street, Oxford OX2 6DP
Oxford University Press is a department of the University of Oxford.
It furthers the University's objective of excellence in research, scholarship,
and education by publishing worldwide in

Oxford New York

Auckland Cape Town Dar es Salaam Hong Kong Karachi
Kuala Lumpur Madrid Melbourne Mexico City Nairobi
New Delhi Shanghai Taipei Toronto

With offices in

Argentina Austria Brazil Chile Czech Republic France Greece
Guatemala Hungary Italy Japan Poland Portugal Singapore
South Korea Switzerland Thailand Turkey Ukraine Vietnam

OXFORD and OXFORD ENGLISH are registered trade marks of
Oxford University Press in the UK and in certain other countries

© Oxford University Press 2011
The moral rights of the author have been asserted
Database right Oxford University Press (maker)
First published 2011
2015 2014 2013 2012 2011
10 9 8 7 6 5 4 3 2 1

No unauthorized photocopying

All rights reserved. No part of this publication may be reproduced, stored
in a retrieval system, or transmitted, in any form or by any means, without
the prior permission in writing of Oxford University Press, or as expressly
permitted by law, by licence or under terms agreed with the appropriate
reprographics rights organization. Enquiries concerning reproduction outside
the scope of the above should be sent to the ELT Rights Department, Oxford
University Press, at the address above

You must not circulate this work in any other form and you must impose
this same condition on any acquirer

Links to third party websites are provided by Oxford in good faith and for
information only. Oxford disclaims any responsibility for the materials
contained in any third party website referenced in this work

ISBN: 978 0 19 464575 1

Printed in China
This book is printed on paper from certified and well-managed sources

ACKNOWLEDGEMENTS
Earth Then and Now Activity Book by: Alistair McCallum
Illustrations by: Kelly Kennedy, Ian Moores, and Alan Rowe

Introduction ← Page 3

1 Circle the correct words.

1 Earth formed **thousands** / **millions** / **billions** of years ago.
2 Earth is a **star** / **planet** / **moon**.
3 Earth has **changed a little** / **changed a lot** / **stayed the same** since it formed.
4 The continents **have moved** / **haven't moved** / **have gone** since Earth first formed.
5 **Some** / **All** / **None** of the animals on Earth have been here for a very long time.
6 Scientists think that people have been on Earth for about **two thousand** / **two hundred thousand** / **two million** years.

2 Answer the questions.

1 Which continent is your country in?

_____

2 Where did the first people on Earth live?

_____

3 How many people live on Earth now?

_____

4 How do you think people have changed Earth? (Write two ways.)

_____

_____

1 A Ball of Fire ← Pages 4–7

1 Write the words. Then complete the sentences.

e_rco _____   n_el_mat _____

d_is_sn^al _____   t_ru_cs _____

v_aal _____   g_am_am _____

1 Earth's __core__ is at the center of the planet.

2 Earth's surface is a layer of solid rock called the _____.

3 Under Earth's crust, there's a layer called the _____.

4 The mantle is mostly made of liquid rock, called _____.

5 When magma gets to Earth's surface, it's called _____.

6 Iceland and Hawaii are volcanic _____.

2 Circle the correct words.

1 Earth's mantle is very **cold** / **hot** / **cool**.

2 Earth's core is mostly made of **iron** / **gold** / **water** and nickel.

3 Earth's crust is usually about **3** / **30** / **300** kilometers thick.

4 Lava comes out of holes in volcanoes called **vents** / **cones** / **eruptions**.

5 Pillow lava is formed under **mountains** / **clouds** / **the ocean**.

6 In 2010, a volcano in Iceland erupted and produced big clouds of **water** / **dust** / **ash**.

7 After the eruption in Iceland in 2010, thousands of people couldn't **watch TV** / **travel** / **eat**.

3 Order the words. Then write *true* or *false*.

1 enormous / planet / fire. / Our / started / ball / as / of / an
   <u>Our planet started as an enormous ball of fire.</u>   <u>true</u>

2 Earth / about / years old. / Scientists / 4.6 million / is / think that
   _____   _____

3 about / old. / in / The Great Pyramid / is / 4,600 years / Egypt
   _____   _____

4 at the bottom / thicker / the ocean. / crust / is / Earth's / of
   _____   _____

5 the part / The mantle / on. / is / we live / of Earth / that
   _____   _____

6 volcanic / under / vents / the ocean. / Sometimes / form
   _____   _____

4 Complete the sentences.

1 Scientists think that Earth was formed from a c_____ of gas, dust, and rock.

2 Earth started as a ball of fire and l_____ rock.

3 Earth's inner core is s_____, because the other layers push down on it with incredible p_____.

4 At first, the t_____ on Earth's surface was very hot.

5 Earth's core is mostly made of two m_____.

6 When a volcano e_____, it produces lava.

5

2 Water and Air (Pages 8–11)

1 **Write the words.**

1 <u>o c e a n</u>   2 _ _ _ _ _   3 _ _ _ _ _

4 _ _ _ _ _ _ _   5 _ _ _ _   6 _ _ _ _

2 **Number the sentences in order (1 = first, 6 = last).**

1 Earth started to cool down. ☐

2 Liquid water covered most of our planet's surface. ☐

3 There was lots of water vapor in the atmosphere. ☐

4 Water vapor came from inside the planet when volcanoes erupted. ☐ 1

5 It started to rain. ☐

6 The water vapor condensed and formed clouds. ☐

3 Match. Then write sentences.

The water in our oceans is — about 3.5% salt.
Today, water covers — about 70% of our planet.
Billions of years ago, — Earth's surface was dry.
Today, the air that we breathe is — about 21% oxygen.
No plants or animals can live — in Lake Assal.
Only 3% of Earth's water is — fresh water.

1 The water in our oceans is about 3.5% salt.
2 Today, water covers about 70% of our planet.
3 Billions of years ago, Earth's surface was dry.
4 Today, the air that we breathe is about 21% oxygen.
5 No plants or animals can live in Lake Assal.
6 Only 3% of Earth's water is fresh water.

4 Complete the sentences.

fossils   oxygen   living   sunlight   ~~billion~~
atmosphere   pools   bacteria

About 3 __billion__ years ago, __living__ things appeared on Earth. Some of the first living things were tiny blue-green __bacteria__. They grew in shallow __pools__ of warm water. We can find their __fossils__ today. They used __sunlight__, water, and carbon dioxide to make their own food. They also produced __oxygen__, and after millions of years there was lots of oxygen in Earth's oceans and __atmosphere__.

3 Minerals and Rock ← Pages 12–15

1 Complete the sentences.

1 Pumice can f_____ on water.

2 Rocks with c_____ inside are called geodes.

3 Granite and obsidian are examples of i_____ rock.

4 The Giant's Causeway formed during volcanic e_____ more than 60 million years ago.

5 There are about 40,000 tall c_____ in the Giant's Causeway.

6 Scientists often find f_____ of dead plants and animals between different l_____ of sediment.

2 Order the words.

1 three / are / types / rock. / of / There

_____

2 cause / and wind / erosion. / can / Water

_____

3 about / rock / tell / Sedimentary / us / can / past. / Earth's

_____

4 at the bottom / forms / often / of oceans. / layers / Sediment

_____

5 more / years old. / fossils / are / Some / 500 million / than

_____

3 Complete the sentences.

1 Earth's crust is solid rock that's _made of minerals._
2 Amethyst crystals form in holes inside _____
3 Igneous rock forms when hot magma and lava cool down and _____
4 Sedimentary rock is interesting because it can tell us about _____
5 Metamorphic rock is sedimentary rock or igneous rock that has changed because of lots of _____
6 Marble is good for _____

4 Write the words. Then answer the questions.

> Where   How many   ~~What~~   When   What

1 _What_ is rock made of?
   It's made of minerals.

2 _____ types of rock are there?
   _____

3 _____ is the Giant's Causeway?
   _____

4 _____ can cause erosion?
   _____

5 _____ can sedimentary rock and igneous rock change into metamorphic rock?
   _____

4 Tectonic Plates Pages 16–19

1 Match. Then write sentences.

Tectonic plates	see	away from each other.
Earth's crust	form	divided into enormous pieces.
We sometimes	move	together like a puzzle.
Sometimes tectonic plates	fit	under oceans.
Mountains can	is	folds in the sides of hills.

1 Tectonic plates fit together like a puzzle.
2 _____
3 _____
4 _____
5 _____

2 Complete the sentences.

1 One tectonic plate can push another plate down into Earth's m a n t l e, where it _ _ _ _ _ and changes into magma.

2 Earth's crust can _ _ _ _ _ and fold.

3 When tectonic plates _ _ _ _ together too hard or too quickly, they break into large _ _ _ _ _ _ of rock.

4 If an earthquake happens _ _ _ _ _ _ _ _ _ _ _, it can make a giant wave, called a _ _ _ _ _ _ _.

5 The Mid-Atlantic Rift goes down the _ _ _ _ _ _ of the Atlantic _ _ _ _ _ _, from the Arctic to Antarctica.

3 Write the words. Then complete the sentences.

a m g a m _____   e n t s i n c o n t _____

t i r f _____   u m o t i n n a s _____

q u a e a r t e k h s _____   c e c t i n o t _____

1 Earth's crust is divided into enormous pieces, called _____ plates.

2 Today, the land on Earth is divided into _____, with seas and oceans between them.

3 Tectonic plates float on the _____ in Earth's mantle.

4 Sometimes two tectonic plates meet and push each other up to create new _____.

5 Sometimes tectonic plates move away from each other and make a _____.

6 When Earth's crust moves suddenly, it can cause _____.

4 Complete the sentences.

> 76 million   10   6,962   1.1 billion   10,000

1 About _____ years ago, most of the land on Earth formed a giant continent called Rodinia.

2 The Mid-Atlantic Rift is about _____ kilometers long.

3 Tectonic plates move about _____ centimeters every year.

4 The Andes Mountains are about _____ years old.

5 The highest mountain in the Andes is _____ meters high.

5 Plant Life ← Pages 20–23

1 **Write the words.**

1 m_____   2 spore c_____
3 f_____   4 f_____
5 n_____   6 c_____
7 l_____   8 f_____
9 f_____   10 s_____

2 **Circle the correct words.**

1 The wind and insects **grow / produce / pollinate** flowering plants.

2 New flowering plants grow from **cones / seeds / spores**.

3 Ferns have long leaves called **fronds / needles / branches**.

4 Conifers grow their seeds inside **capsules / cones / flowers** to keep them safe.

5 **Flowering plants / Ferns / Conifers** give us rice, vegetables, and fruit.

3 Correct the sentences.

1 The first plants on Earth lived on the mountains.
   <u>The first plants on Earth lived in the ocean.</u>

2 The first land plants were seed plants, like mosses.
   _____

3 The first land plants grew in hot places near water.
   _____

4 Conifers were shorter than ferns, so they got more sunlight.
   _____

5 The oldest living things on Earth today are ferns.
   _____

6 Today, about 8% of the plants on Earth are flowering plants.
   _____

4 Complete the sentences.

> oxygen   canopy   conifers   tropical   medicines   deciduous

1 In cold climates, most trees are _____ that stay green all year long.

2 In warmer climates, there are _____ trees that grow new leaves in spring.

3 In hot climates, there are often _____ rainforests.

4 In rainforests, the tallest trees form the _____ at the top.

5 Plants in rainforests produce lots of _____.

6 Scientists can make _____ from many plants that grow in rainforests.

6 Animal Life ← Pages 24–27

1 **Order the words. Then answer the questions.**

1 the first animals / did / in the ocean? / When / appear

   <u>When did the first animals appear in the ocean?</u>
   <u>They appeared more than 700 million years ago.</u>

2 crabs and jellyfish / do / live? / Where

   _____
   _____

3 the first / appear? / When / fish / did

   _____
   _____

4 from water? / How / fish / oxygen / do / take

   _____
   _____

5 do / What / produce? / mammal mothers

   _____
   _____

2 **Complete the sentences.**

1 The first animals were very _ _ _ _ _ _ living things.

2 Invertebrates are animals with no _ _ _ _ _ _ _ _ _.

3 All fish have _ _ _ _ _ to take oxygen from water.

4 The dinosaurs lived on Earth for about 150 million years, before they became _ _ _ _ _ _ _ _.

3 Write the words. Then complete the chart.

1 ʳₐdᵤlₛi _lizards_
2 ᵖhiᵈolⁿˢ _____
3 ⁿiᵖⁿeᵍuₛ _____
4 ₐₙkₑₛₛ _____
5 ᵖₒlᵖₑₑ _____
6 ʳₒₛtiʰₑₛc _____
7 ˢhʳₒₑₛ _____
8 cₑrᵢcᵒdₛₒl _____

Reptiles	Birds	Mammals
lizards	_____	_____
_____	_____	_____
_____		_____

4 Order the words.

1 Earth's / Fish / vertebrates. / were / first
_____

2 fins / to swim. / have / and a tail / fish / to help them / Most
_____

3 protect / scales / have / their skin. / Reptiles / to
_____

4 more mammals / became extinct, / appeared. / the dinosaurs / When
_____

5 can / that / are / the / Bats / mammals / fly. / only
_____

15

 Temperature Pages 28–31

1 **Write the words.**

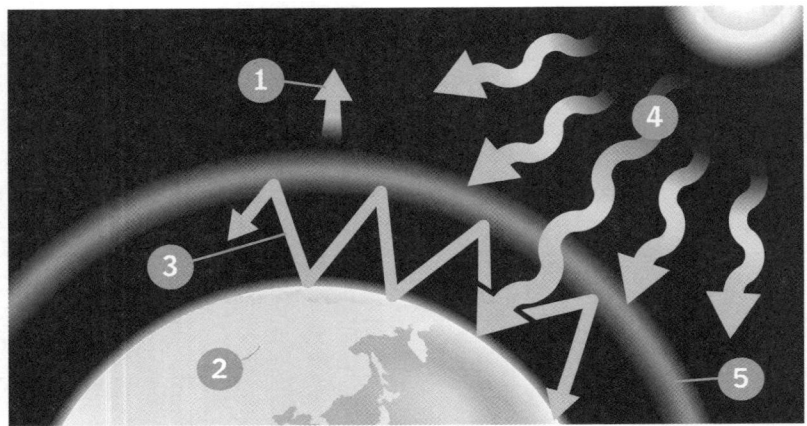

1 some heat _ _ _ _ _ _ _ _   2 _ _ _ _ _ _

3 some heat is _ _ _ _ _ _ _ _   4 heat from the _ _ _

5 _ _ _ _ _ _ _ _ _ _ _ gases

2 **Match. Then write sentences.**

Earth's temperature has changed	long valleys.
The last ice age ended	in Antarctica.
The world's largest glacier is	more than 10,000 years ago.
When glaciers move, they cut	many times.
The greenhouse effect keeps	Earth warm.

1 _____
2 _____
3 _____
4 _____
5 _____

3 Order the words. Then answer the questions.

1 glaciers / Can / very / big? / become
   Can glaciers become very big?
   Yes, they can.

2 form / Do / quickly? / glaciers
   _____
   _____

3 always been / temperature / Has / the same? / Earth's
   _____
   _____

4 the sun? / get / Does / from / Earth / heat
   _____
   _____

5 during / Do / grow well / greenhouse periods? / plants
   _____
   _____

4 Complete the sentences.

During ice ages, Earth's t_____ is very cold for a long time. Winters become colder and longer, and large glaciers f_____, especially at Earth's P_____. This happens because the Poles get less s_____ than other places on Earth. Glaciers r_____ lots of sunlight into space, which makes Earth's temperature much c_____.

8 People on Earth ← Pages 32–35

1 Match. Then write sentences.

Early people lived
We need to care
People have changed
Water and air are
We burn fossil fuels
Oil, coal, and gas are

to produce energy.
for natural areas.
renewable resources.
non-renewable resources.
in Africa.
our planet in many ways.

1 _____
2 _____
3 _____
4 _____
5 _____
6 _____

2 Circle the correct words.

1 In **urban** / **rural** / **natural** areas, farmers have cleared land to grow crops.

2 Rainforests and national parks are **urban** / **rural** / **natural** areas.

3 Earth gives us **water** / **air** / **oil** to breathe.

4 We can get renewable **energy** / **food** / **gas** from the sun and the wind.

5 Metals are **plant** / **fossil** / **mineral** resources that we use to make products in factories.

6 We need to use oil, coal, and gas **quickly** / **carefully** / **badly**.

3 Write the words. Then answer the questions.

> Why   How   What   How many   Why   Where

1 _____ are natural areas important?

_____

2 _____ people live on Earth?

_____

3 _____ did people live 200,000 years ago?

_____

4 _____ can we reduce the amount of waste that we produce?

_____

5 _____ have people built in urban areas?

_____

6 _____ do we need to use oil and gas carefully?

_____

4 Complete the sentences.

> greenhouse   carbon   smoke   waste   planet   fuels

1 We throw away too much _____.
2 Our cars and factories produce _____ that pollutes the air.
3 Scientists think that a new _____ period is starting.
4 For 150 years, people have burned lots of fossil _____.
5 We need to produce less _____ dioxide.
6 We live on a beautiful _____ that has been here for billions of years.

After Reading — Pages 3–35

1 **Check your answers to Activity 1, page 3.**

1 = billions   2 = planet   3 = changed a lot
4 = have moved   5 = Some   6 = two hundred thousand

2 **Complete the puzzle.**

1 Volcanoes produce ___ when they erupt.
2 ___ is liquid rock.
3 Glaciers ___ in warm weather.
4 Frogs and toads are ___.
5 Iceland is a ___ island.
6 Mammals produce ___ for their babies.
7 Trees use ___ dioxide.
8 ___ plates float on magma.
9 ___ have no backbone.
10 We burn coal to produce ___.
11 There is iron and ___ in Earth's core.
12 The first plants lived in the ___.
13 Earth gets heat from the ___.
14 Seven ___ people live on Earth.

20

3 Write the words. Then find and write the page.

1 We live on this part of Earth.   _crust_   _page 5_
2 These were Earth's first seed plants.   _____   _____
3 These are the only mammals that can fly.   _____   _____
4 We couldn't live without this gas in the air.   _____   _____
5 These get less sunlight than other places on Earth.   _____   _____
6 This type of rock is good for making statues.   _____   _____
7 When Earth's crust moves very suddenly, it can cause these.   _____   _____
8 All fish use these to take oxygen from the water.   _____   _____
9 Scientists often find fossils in this type of rock.   _____   _____
10 This rock can float on water.   _____   _____
11 This was a giant continent about 1.1 billion years ago.   _____   _____
12 Scientists can make these from many plants that grow in rainforests.   _____   _____

4 Complete the sentences.

1 Conifers are __taller than__ ferns. They are __the oldest__ living things on Earth. (tall / old)

2 The Amazon Rainforest is _____ tropical rainforest in the world. (big)

3 Earth is one million times _____ the Great Pyramid. (old)

4 The dinosaurs are _____ reptiles in history. (famous)

5 Amethyst crystals are _____ granite crystals. (big)

6 The Burgess Shale fossil field is one of _____ places in the world for finding fossils. (good)

5 Write the words. Then answer the questions.

Are   Did   Could   ~~Do~~   Can   Is   Has   Was

1 __Do__ volcanoes produce lots of ash? __Yes, they do.__

2 _____ Earth's core made of metal? _____

3 _____ there any liquid water on Earth at first?

_____

4 _____ we live without oxygen? _____

5 _____ our oceans salty? _____

6 _____ some rocks float on water? _____

7 _____ the first animals appear in forests? _____

8 _____ Earth's temperature always been the same?

_____

6 Complete the chart. Then write two sentences about people.

> giant million ~~surface~~ species 80% continents
> cool covers flowering ~~liquid~~ divided mammals
> 70% ocean mosses billion

Water	**Then**: At first, there wasn't any ___liquid___ water on Earth's __surface__. **Now**: Water _____ about _____ of our planet.
Land	**Then**: About one _____ years ago, there was a _____ continent called Rodinia. **Now**: Land on Earth is _____ into smaller _____, with seas and oceans between them.
Plants	**Then**: The first land plants were non-seed plants, like _____, that grew in _____ places near water. **Now**: About _____ of the plants on Earth are _____ plants.
Animals	**Then**: The first animals appeared in the _____ more than 700 _____ years ago. **Now**: There are thousands of _____ of fish, amphibians, reptiles, birds, and _____.
People	**Then**: _____ _____ **Now**: _____

 # My Book Review

Earth Then and Now

Title of this book: _____

Name of the author: _____

This book is about _____ in the past and today.

Questions about this book

1 What new words did you learn from this book? (Write six words.)
   _____
   _____

2 What types of rock did you learn about? (Write two types.)
   _____

3 Write one plant and one animal from the book.
   _____

4 Which places in the book would you like to visit?
   _____

What I like about this book

My favorite chapter was _____.

My favorite picture was _____.

My scores for this book (draw ☺, ☺☺, or ☺☺☺)

Interesting book ◯◯◯   Interesting cover ◯◯◯

Interesting pictures ◯◯◯   Fun to read ◯◯◯

Which book do you want to read next? _____